Survival Shelter:

Build Your Storm Shelter and Root Cellar To Survive In Any Situation

and sourced from Flickr

The information herein is offered for informational purposes solely, and is universal as so. The presentation of the information is without contract or any type of guarantee assurance.

The trademarks that are used are without any consent, and the publication of the trademark is without permission or backing by the trademark owner. All trademarks and brands within this book are for clarifying purposes only and are the owned by the owners themselves, not affiliated with this document.

Table of Contents

Introduction

It is not hard to imagine what might have been going through the minds of the residents of Joplin, Missouri during the late afternoon of May 22nd, 2011. When one of the biggest tornadoes in US history cut a 1½-mile slice through the southwestern part of the city many were caught unaware and completely unprepared. Starting in the early evening, a tornado touched down and quickly escalated to a category 5 storm packing winds of more than 300 mph.

Residents throughout the city had to stop whatever they were doing and run for cover. Sadly however, many who sought cover quickly learned that their chosen place of refuge was not adequate enough for the baseball sized hail, powerful winds, and falling debris.

Twenty minutes later, the tornado finally left leaving behind a section of the city scattered with bodies and total devastation in its wake. The final tally, 161 dead, over 1000 injured, and more than 9,000 people left homeless.

Within months, many survivors who had counted themselves lucky to have made it through the disaster began making plans to build their own storm shelters so they could be better prepared the next time a tragedy strikes.

Disasters come in all forms and can happen anywhere in this world. People on the west coast are drilled constantly about earthquake preparedness whereas those in the Midwest are often deeply concerned about tornadoes. Those on the east coast brace themselves for hurricanes every year and in the northeast, threat of blizzards, extremely cold temperatures, and dangers from ice are more common.

Then there are also those disasters that can happen at any time and any place. Fires, floods, drought, and more are often in the back of our consciousness even when things are going well.

It's been drilled into our heads from childhood, that being prepared for a disaster is the key to surviving one. So, when a tornado or hurricane is imminent in your area, a flood of questions immediately comes to your mind.

- Where will you run for shelter?
- How far is it?
- How long will it take to get there?
- What about the family?
- Do you have enough supplies?

The answers to these questions are actually so important that your survival and that of your family rests on them. When a disaster strikes, you may have only seconds to make decisions that could actually buy years for those you care about. This is why so many people choose to be proactive and prepare for these events well in advance by building a storm shelter or a safe room, a place where they can run to for protection.

Through the pages of this book we hope to give you the guidelines to help you to decide how to build your own storm shelter and what you need to know. By the time you finish reading these pages, we hope you'll be better able to decide if you have the skills and know-how to build your own shelter or if you should hire professionals to do it. You'll also know about the different options for shelters and the advantages and disadvantages you have with each one.

We hope that once you finish reading these pages, you'll feel more confident and better prepared for whatever may come up in the future. While there is no guarantee that a shelter will be the sole reason for your survival in the face of disaster, it can certain increase your odds and give you peace of mind at the same time.

Chapter 1 – Why You Need a Storm Shelter/Root Cellar

I Every year, we all understand that storm season will come and while we may not know where the devastation will hit, we do know that many will be affected somewhere along its path. There is no guarantee that any of us can do anything to avoid impending disaster but our chances of getting through one unscathed is greatly increased by how prepared we may be.

Most people are aware of the need to be prepared for a disaster but unfortunately, because of life in general, we tend to let other things get in the way. As a result we postpone the needed preparations and replace them with other routine tasks that may appear more pressing at the moment.

Another reason some may put off building their storm shelters is because they are unsure of just how to go about it. We are concerned about the value and cost of the project and how difficult it will be to complete. We wonder if there truly a need in the area you live in, and how to be sure that the shelter will be a sound and safe haven in an emergency.

All of these are legitimate questions that deserve an answer. The more informed you are about the topic, the better chances you'll have of getting your needs met when faced with an emergency situation.

As with most locations, there are some regions of the country that will be more heavily impacted by certain disasters than others. So, if you live in a region that is more prone to tornados and powerful storms then you are likely thinking very seriously about building a storm shelter.

Still, regardless to where you live, having some type of safe haven is always a good idea. The question really then should be what type of shelter you need for the type of disasters you are most likely going to face.

Still, there are even more factors you need to consider when deciding to build a storm shelter.

- **Improves Your Property Value**

   Most people are aware that building a storm shelter can be a costly investment. However, there are many financial gains you can achieve if you have one. Yes, there may be a substantial upfront cost but in the end it actually will increase your overall property value.

   Many real estate agents in tornado prone areas estimate that a storm shelter can increase your property value by as much as several thousand dollars. While you may not see an immediate return on your investment, the increase will pay off for you in the end.

- **They are Easy to Build**

Building a storm shelter is not as difficult as one might imagine. In many instances, you can have your shelter in place in just a couple of days. Some have managed to complete a project in as little as a weekend. This fast pace however, will depend largely on having the right expertise, materials, and tools on hand. For the amateur DIYer, it will probably take longer.

- **They are Not Limited to Location**

As you learn more about storm shelters, you'll quickly come to know that there are different types to choose from so deciding you want a shelter is only the first step. They are not limited by either size or location. You can have one as small as a closet in your home or as large your garage.

For many, thoughts of Dorothy pounding her feet at the entrance of her aunt and uncle's underground shelter have concluded that survival is not possible unless the shelter is below ground. But in areas where there is a lot of rocky soil, below ground shelters may not be possible. However, there is a wide variety of shelter designs that can be tailor made for your unique area.

- While all of those are good reasons to build a storm shelter, the most important one is that they save lives. Having the forethought to build one and implement a plan for your family's safety can give you a return far more valuable than the financial gains you may have. There have been many occasions where everything in an area was completely obliterated except for the storm shelter.

- They can serve a dual purpose. Many have found that while these rooms are there to run to for protection, they can also serve other purposes as well. Since the majority of the time, the room will stand empty, many have chosen to convert their storm room into a root cellar so that when there is no impending storm they will still be able to put it to good use. This could be a great place to stock up and store extra food and supplies. As long as the structure is completely sealed off from outside nuisances (spiders, snakes, rodents, etc.) one can actually gain a lot from the use of these small emergency havens.

Preparing for a disaster has become a significant part of our lives, no matter where we live. You may be surprised at just how much peace of mind and comfort you'll have in knowing that your shelter is there to provide you with the protection you need to survive and live another day.

Who Needs a Storm Shelter/Root Cellar?

Most people are fully aware that a storm shelter is essential when you live in areas that are prone to tornados and hurricanes. These small structures are built to withstand winds over 300 mph and to provide protection from any debris that they may picked up and tossed in your direction.

However, few people have come to realize that storm shelters can provide protection in other ways as well. When built according to Federal regulations, these extremely strong and reinforced constructs can also keep other threats away as well. Not only can we seek safety from severe weather conditions but also situations of civil unrest, which often arise in the aftermath of major disasters.

The case of Hurricane Katrina was a perfect example of this. When the storm finally passed over leaving devastation in its wake, hosts of people, frustrated in the slow progress of rescue efforts incited civil unrest and social dangers as well.

Your home may be equipped with alarm systems, motion sensors, and surveillance cameras to warn you of similar threats but you are still highly vulnerable. However, if you have a storm shelter already built with sealed doors, shatter proof windows, and reinforced concrete, you can keep all sorts of unwanted intruders at bay while you wait for help to arrive.

According to statistics released by the FBI, there is one burglary every 10 seconds even when there is no disaster at hand. With nearly nine million property crimes occurring every year, it stands to reason that a storm shelter, which can also double as a safe room can be very beneficial for everyone no matter where they live.

Federal Regulations for Storm Shelters

Now that you understand the value of having a storm shelter in your home can provide you with protection from all sorts of disasters, you need to understand how they provide that protection. We must remember that a storm shelter will be only as good as it is constructed.

This is why FEMA has established certain guidelines to teach us exactly what is needed for a structure to be called a storm shelter and be considered a reasonable place of safety.

What Qualifies as a Storm Shelter?

No structure will be able to provide you with absolute protection from all the threats we face today, however according to the guidelines set out by FEMA, it must provide near-absolute protection. This basically means that the building must be structured based on the current knowledge of disasters like tornados and hurricanes it must withstand.

Every year FEMA releases a publication, FEMA P-361 Safe Rooms for Tornadoes and Hurricanes: Guidance for Community and Residential Safe Rooms and the ICC-500 ICC/NSSA Standard for the Design and Construction of Storm Shelters to keep us up to date.

The publication includes designs and guidelines to follow that can teach you exactly what goes into constructing a storm shelter for your particular location. While you may be able to consult with a contractor or building designer, it is always a good idea to review the design basics and guidelines included.

Because of different threats in different locations, the requirements for building a safe shelter will vary from one place to the next. Differences will also impact where in or around your house is best suited for your shelter, the type of foundation, and the materials needed for construction. It even details information on the type of door you will need.

At the very least, FEMA recommends that your storm shelter is able to withstand winds up to 250 mph and a debris impact of 15lb 2" x 4" board missles traveling horizontally at 100 mph. However, depending on the area for which you live, there may be even more stringent requirements for your shelter to meet before it meets FEMA's approval.

Chapter 2 – Types of DIY Storm Shelters

Once you've made the decision to build your storm shelter you quickly realize that you've just begun. There are a lot more decisions to be made, the first of which is the type of shelter you need. If you live in one of the tornado and hurricane prone regions you might assume that the decision is pretty easy but you'd be mistaken.

Many people assume that an underground shelter is the best way to go but that may not be the best choice for some people. There are different types of shelters that are designed for different soil conditions, climate areas, and water tables. It pays to know the different styles to look at.

Underground Shelter

Sometimes referred to as Earth Shelters, these are usually made from reinforced steel and concrete and are usually built outside and separate from your main living quarters. They can also be installed in the floor of a garage or basement of a home. Underground shelters have walls and ceilings that are completely reinforced and are resistant to extreme winds and the impact that comes from flying debris.

While these shelters are extremely strong and very effective at providing you the protection you need, they may not be easily accessible in an emergency. If a tornado is bearing down on you it may not be safe for you to leave the house you're in to get to the shelter in time.

Another concern with an underground shelter is the risk of being flooded during heavy downpours or your sole exit from the shelter could be blocked by falling debris leaving you trapped inside.

Partial Home Build and Above Ground Shelters

In some areas, the water table is so high underground shelters are not possible. In these areas, a partial home build or an above ground shelter is constructed as a viable alternative. These look very much like a bank safe with extra fortification. They are usually made with reinforced concrete or steel.

When not in use, they can be made into a storage room or a closet. Regardless of how they are used, in order for them to withstand the pressures of the elements, they need to be completely self-contained and anchored to the home's foundation.

Above ground shelters can be made a part of the existing home structure or they can stand separate from the home wherever easy access is possible.

One of the biggest drawbacks to a partial home build is the amount of space it can take inside your home.

With above-ground shelters, you may also have the risk of the entryway being blocked by falling debris. In such cases, design features like doors opening inward give you a better chance of getting out without being trapped.

There is also some concern that above ground shelters (especially those that stand alone) are not as strong as underground shelters and may not be able to withstand the extreme winds or the flying missiles that may be thrown against it.

Prebuilt Shelter

If you feel you don't have the wherewithal to build your own shelter, there are prebuilt shelters available for purchase. These come in different styles. You can choose from a welded steel box, a steel skeleton for the shell with steel panels on all sides, or one that is completely prefabricated and assembled together at the site.

**How to Decide

Because there are so many designs to choose from it can be difficult to decide which one is right for your situation. The best way to determine which type will work best for you will depend on how much homework you do. You should first learn as much as you can about the weather condition in your area.

According to FEMA, the nation is divided into five different wind zones. Those in Zone 1 are at low risk of needing shelter from an extreme wind. The choice to have a shelter is a matter of preference for the home or business owner. Those in Zone II are at a moderate risk and should consider a shelter for protection from extreme winds.

However for those in Zones III and IV, a shelter or safe room is the preferred method of protection and those in Zone V are in Hurricane prone regions and are considered to be in a high-risk category. In those areas FEMA recommends that all potential safe room occupants comply with local jurisdictional directions and evacuate as an additional alternative to having a storm shelter.

Once you know which Zone of the country you live in, your next step is to learn the soil conditions for your area. This is especially important if you're considering an underground shelter.

In some areas either the water table is too high or the soil conditions will not support a shelter built underground. Knowing this will help you to determine if the type of shelter you want is even possible.

It is also important to factor in your family's unique needs for a shelter. Do you have a small family that could get by with a small, closet sized room or will you need a larger one?

When you're trying to determine the size of the shelter, make sure that you calculate and figure out how much storage space you will need. Once the shelter is built, you need space for storing emergency supplies, food, water, medical equipment, and anything else.

Only after you've figured all of those things in, consider the cost. There is a saying, "Knowledge is Power," the more you inform yourself about your needs and your options, the easier it will be to decide which shelter is the best for you.

Chapter 3 – Supplies & Materials

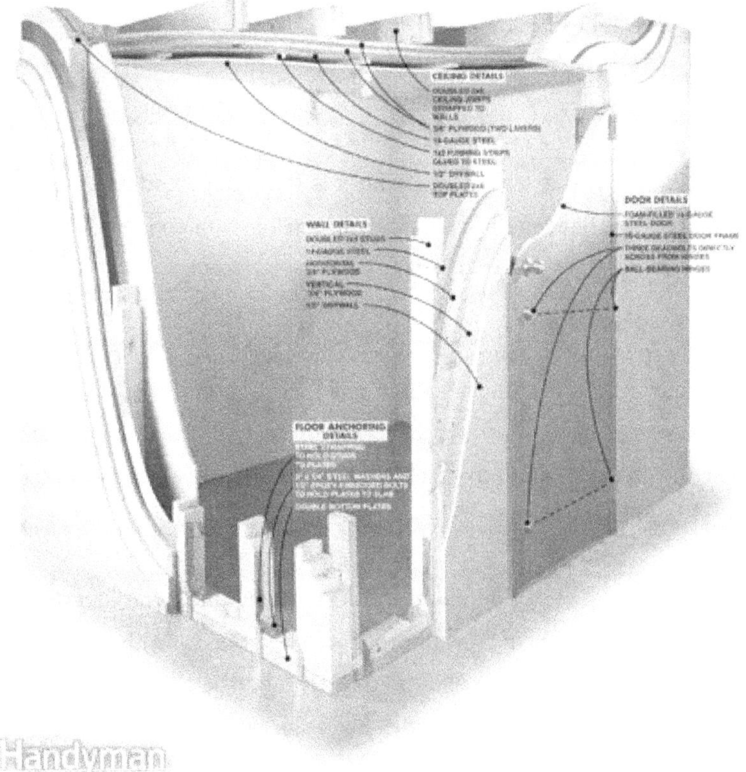

Now that you've decided on the type of storm shelter you need, you're ready to get started. One of the first things you need to do is to obtain the materials needed for your shelter's construction.

You might think that concrete is the best option because it is so strong and resistant but with modern technology, there are quite a few other options that can prove just as strong.

Concrete: One of the reasons concrete is used so much in storm shelters is its availability. It is easy to get and it is far more affordable than other materials. The challenge of building your shelter with concrete however is because as heavy and strong as it is – it is also porous.

This means that eventually water will seep through it. In a severe hurricane you may find yourself with protection from the wind and projectiles flying through the air but having to live knee deep in water.

Fiberglass: Another option that is also quite affordable but has the added benefit of being waterproof is fiberglass. With the proper reinforcements, it is strong enough to withstand the gale force winds but not as heavy as the concrete. It does have one major drawback and that is the material has a tendency to "sweat," which can lead to other problems like mold buildup on the walls.

To prevent this, it is important for you to clean and paint the shelter on a regular basis to stay ahead of the problem. You may also have to worry about the vacuum pressure, which can literally pull a fiberglass shelter out of the ground if it is not bolted down and firmly secured to a concrete foundation.

Galvanized Steel: Because steel is one of the most durable materials available, you can expect that your shelter could last a lifetime. It doesn't require a great deal of maintenance and it is incredibly strong. However, steel is also the most costly of materials for building. Considering the extra strength you will get and the fact that it will last for generations, you may find it is well worth the investment.

Combination: Some of the strongest storm shelters built today consist of a combination of materials. Imagine a galvanized steel shelter covered in zinc and then encased in concrete.

Fittings

On the surface, you may feel that a storm shelter is just a concrete foundation, maybe some poured concrete with some rebar to give it strength but it is much more than that. If you want it to pass FEMA inspection, your shelter will require more than 100 different parts and must fit together like a giant jigsaw puzzle.

There are several websites online where you can purchase shelter designs giving you the exact number of bolts, fasteners, bearings, locks, doors, nuts, and more that you may need. Not to mention a collection of the proper tools necessary to put it all together.

Equipment

Finally, you'll need to have the proper equipment to get the job done. Building a shelter, while it can be a DIY project, is a heavy-duty adventure. At the very least you will need to rent some heavy equipment to even get started. In most cases, you'll need a concrete vibrator, a diamond blade, a dump truck, a Georgia buggy, a hydraulic rock hammer, mini excavator, pressure washer, and a wet saw.

Once you've gathered all your supplies and equipment together, you are ready to start building. Remember, your storm shelter is going to be a life-saving resource for you and your family so unless you have specialized skills in working with construction of this type it might be worthwhile to consider hiring at least one professional to make sure that everything will be done according to the specifications laid out by FEMA. It may cost you more up front but amateur work could have a major impact on the strength and durability of the finished shelter.

Chapter 4 – Steps to Building

If you have purchased designs for your storm shelter then the step-by-step instructions are already included. While shelters may vary, the order of construction is pretty similar across the board. Underground shelters are often more difficult to construct and you will need to include a ventilation system to ensure that you don't cut off your air supply when inside.

One way around this is by constructing what is called a "Berm Shelter," which is a slight variation of the underground shelter. Most of the structure is below ground but the roof remains just above the ground level.

Basic Steps in Building a Berm Shelter

To build a Berm Shelter, you will first need to excavate a pit large enough to hold the entire shelter and a little room to work around the exterior while you are working.

Next, you will have to lay and pour a concrete foundation, which will also serve as the floor of your shelter.

Once the foundation has been laid, a wooden frame is built out of plywood to create a mold for pouring the concrete walls and roof. The concrete needs to be reinforced with wire mesh and rebar to give the shelter added strength.

After the walls have been poured, preparing for the installation of the door is next. The door should have a steel frame and open inward. This provides additional protection so you won't be trapped inside.

The finishing touches could include adding some aesthetics to help it to blend in with the landscape or to make it more waterproof.

Basic Steps in Building an Underground Shelter

Below ground shelters are usually found outside of the main building structure, but they can also be built underneath the main living quarters.

Begin by excavating a pit that is large enough to hold the shelter with enough room to work around it.

Create a concrete foundation that will also serve as the floor of the shelter.

To erect the walls you have several options. First, you could begin with constructing a sturdy wooden frame inside the pit and a membrane made of waterproof material. Once the frame and the membrane is in place, pour your concrete, which can be reinforced with wire mesh or metal sheets and secure it to both the frame and the floor.

Ideally, if you have more experience you could build one long wall of welded steel and wrap it around the frame. Both methods will give you the type of shelter you need. Whatever you decide, always follow the specifications that come with your designs and make sure you meet any FEMA regulations that apply.

Once the walls are in place, attention should be given to your ventilation system. Without this, conditions may become unbearable. When you first enter a shelter, it is usually pretty cool but once you've been enclosed in one for several days, you'll notice the temperature will make a drastic change.

The floors, walls, and the ceiling will slowly absorb the body heat of everyone inside and before long the temperature inside will increase to dangerous levels.

The ventilation system you choose should be able to pull air in from the outside without bringing in any debris or extreme winds from the weather. There are several ways to do this.

1.Use an air pump. These usually come with very specific installation instructions

2.Another option is to allow for natural ventilation. If you have openings that are large enough on opposite sides of the shelter, a consistent airflow will naturally come in. However, that is only if there is any breeze flowing from the outside.

3. If the air is hot and still, you won't get any flow of fresh air in your shelter. You could also create a chimney like opening in the ceiling and create an opposite opening near the floor of the shelter. When this works, the warmer air will rise to the ceiling and escape through the chimney while a flow of cooler air will come in through the floor. However, if the shelter is going to be occupied by several people this option may not be adequate enough to maintain a comfortable air temperature.

4. A third option is to purchase a ventilation system and install it according to the manufacturers instructions. This way, you can be sure that your system will perform exactly as expected and be able

to accommodate the number of people you plan to have in your shelter.

5. There is also the Direction fanning method, which involves using a manual pump to bring fresh air into a shelter. These devices are relatively simple to make with easily attainable materials and can work well on small shelters that only need to support a few people. Instructions on how to build one can come with the basic designs you purchase for your shelter.

When you give your attention to installing a door on your shelter there are several things that need to be kept in mind. Doors need to be strong enough to withstand powerful missles hurled at it at speeds that exceed 100 mph.

This will require a steel frame and a door that is strong enough to withstand the external pressures but not so heavy that it would be difficult to open and close in a hurry.

Once the door is secured, the exterior roof of the shelter should be built. This should be made from a single slab of reinforced concrete and should be thick and strong enough to withstand the pressure of at least 200lb/ square foot.

These are all basic instructions for building a storm shelter. Because there are so many variations on shelters, materials to use, and location concerns it is important that you follow the guidelines included with your specific designs.

Anyone can dig a hole in their backyard and fill it with concrete but if you want your shelter to gain FEMA approval, it is always best to use a professional designer and contractor to work with you through each phase of the building project. They know exactly what will be needed in your area and what will be the best way to get your shelter approved.

Chapter 5 – The Finishing Touches

We've discussed several varieties of storm shelters with the single goal of preparing for an impending disaster of some kind. But if you limit your storm shelter to only one function it could be an incredible disservice. While their primary purpose is to protect you from harm, they can easily do double duty in a variety of ways.

You basically have a practically hermetically sealed room than can be used for many things. Many people have found that using their shelter as a root cellar is probably one of the best uses for the room. Think about it.

The room is completely sealed away from snakes, spiders, rodents, and other natural predators that are looking for a quick and easy meal. It is waterproof, and if you have a proper ventilation system installed it is also kept at the ideal temperature so you can preserve food. All of this was in addition to its ability to protect you from severe environmental conditions.

Basically, a root cellar is just a cool and dark place to store food and root vegetables. It needs to be dark and dry for the best results. If you plan to use your storm shelter as a root cellar you should implement this in your design plan from the very beginning. Some people prefer to have a storm shelter with two separate rooms.

The first room will be used as the actual shelter and the second room, which is hidden from view behind a secret door is used as the root cellar.

If you choose this plan, you must accommodate for the extra space from the very beginning of the project. Once the pit is excavated, make sure that you lay out a foundation that will support both rooms. While you'll lay a concrete foundation for the storm shelter, the root cellar usually works best with an earthen floor.

When you build your walls, make sure that you leave space to accommodate your ventilation system. You can do this with cinder blocks, reinforced rebar and wire mesh, and fill all openings with concrete.

Once the walls are finished, top them with a one-inch thick wooden frame.

The type of door you use will depend largely on where your shelter will be. For those who build under their home or garage, creating a hidden entryway inside the house would be the best option. Some have built them under the stairs while others build them with trap doors somewhere in the house. The decision will be dependent on how convenient it will be to access in the case of an emergency.

The entrance to your root cellar should be sealed enough to trap the cool air inside and maintain a constant temperature.

Install shelving as needed for your cellar. Make sure to avoid pressure treated wood as it can eventually put out off-gasses and toxins into the enclosed environment.

That wouldn't be good for your health or the food you plan to store. Make sure that the shelving and foodstuffs you stock are kept at least six inches from the walls. This helps to keep the air circulation constant.

Root cellars also need to have their doors and roofing insulated. Installing insulator board over the surfaces can do this.

You are now ready to stock up your root cellar and your storm shelter so you are fully prepared for an emergency.

Stocking the Root Cellar

It is important to understand that while root cellars are cooler, the temperature inside can fluctuate with the seasons, so it is not good to store foods that will perish quickly.

If you have installed a system to control the climate you'll have more options of foods to store. When storing for the winter there are several rules you should keep in mind.

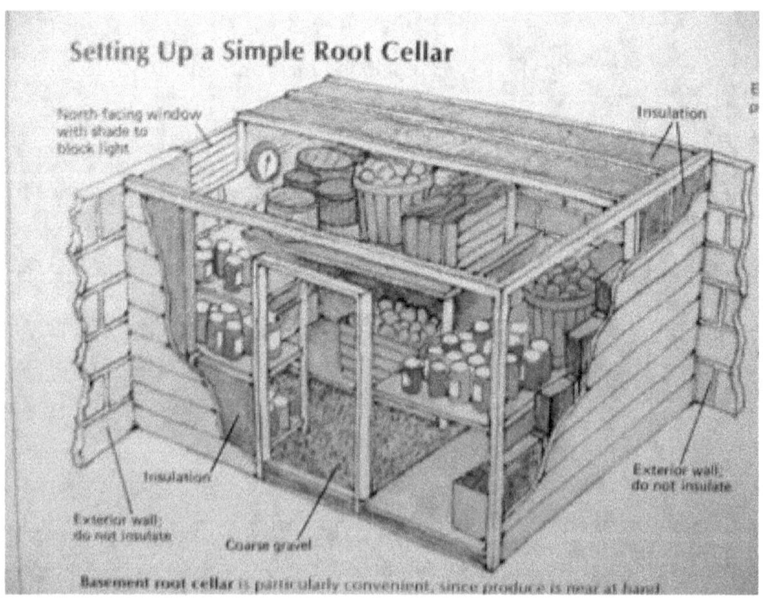

1. Treat them gently so they don't bruise. Bruised vegetables will go bad much faster.
2. Pick your produce when it is mature. Don't store anything that is not yet ripened or is overripe.
3. Store during a dry spell.

4. Choose only those vegetables that will adapt well to storage. These include beets, cabbage, potatoes, and carrots or foods like these.
5. Once the food is picked, chill immediately before storing in the root cellar.
6. Trim off the green tops leaving about an inch of stub but don't cut off the tops or break the skin.

By following these basic guidelines you can ensure that the foods you store will last much longer than they would normally be expected to.

You can also store in your root cellar extra supplies of water, canned and preserved foods, dry grains, beans, onions, and similar items.

Because it will have a cooler temperature, it may also be a good idea to store extra medicines that you might need in case of an emergency.

Stocking Your Storm Shelter

When it comes to food, the same basic rules apply when stocking your storm shelter. Perishable items will deteriorate quickly so make sure you stock more canned and preserved goods than perishables.

It is always wise to err on the side of caution so stock up with more water than you think you'll need. Estimate at least three gallons of water a day for each person and at least enough food to last a week for each person.

When you think of your shelter as a camping site, it is easy to understand what equipment you might need. If you don't have bunks installed inside you'll need sleeping bags or fold up camping beds, portable lights, cooking gear, pillows, blankets, pots and pans for cooking, dishes, etc.

For emergency equipment you'll need an NOAA Radio, flashlights, propane gas tanks, cell phone, and extra batteries. A First Aid Kit with material for treating emergencies like cuts, sprains, bruises, and other injuries and medicines for treating common ailments like fever, cold, cough, or the flu. This is especially important if anyone will be in the shelter that requires constant medication.

Make sure that everything is stored in watertight containers. Especially things like candles and matches so that they will be useful when you need them.

There are lots of things that can be stored in the storm shelter and root cellar. There are likely many things not listed here that you might want to have close at hand in case of an emergency.

Conclusion

All of us know that we could be facing a disaster at any moment. Whether it is from the earth's natural forces or manmade, have a safe haven to run to in an emergency gives us all peace of mind and comfort. We have a plan and we know what to do.

Having a shelter can be a costly investment but the returns you get from it do not come in the form of dollars and cents. It comes in the form of safety for our loved ones and the years we gain to be with them.

We hope that you have learned enough through these pages to build your own storm shelter so you can have safety in the face of imminent danger. By gaining this basic knowledge, you will be one step closer to protecting your family in ways that truly matter to all of us.